HER WORKS PRAISE HER

HER
WORKS
PRAISE
HER

A STUDY COURSE FOR WOMEN

By Jeannette Nichols

We are proud to be able to introduce to the women of the church a book concerning maturing womanhood. In it Jeannette Nichols, a gracious example of that which she writes, brings to us the true meaning of maturity, the art of growing in keeping with our years, our times, and our experiences.

She has written not necessarily to the woman who feels the years are gaining on her but to all women from the teens to the century mark. In her book Sister Nichols has presented the challenge to become a gracious, mature person to every woman who shall read, ponder, and put to use the suggestions offered.

This is a book that has long been needed, a book to be much read, a book to linger long in our thoughts, that it thus may have effect in our lives.

Mrs. J. T. Westwood, Jr., *Director*
General Department of Women

ACKNOWLEDGMENTS

To Aleta Runkle and Kathryn Westwood for reading this manuscript and giving valuable comments.

To Dorothy Fry for lending me material her late husband Evan had compiled on the subject of aging.

To the gracious, good women who inspired the writing of this. Some have passed from this life, but many remain and continue to give good influence.

By their everyday living they have piloted a course — not the easiest — but one which aligned itself with the examples and precepts taught by the Master of earthly relationships.

And to my mother, who left a worthy pattern designed for maturing with grace, I dedicate this writing.

CONTENTS

*W*ho can find a good woman?

She is far more precious than jewels.

The heart of her husband trusts in her.

She will do him good and not evil all the days of her life.

She works with willing hands.

She opens her hand to the poor, and reaches out her hands to the needy.

Strength and dignity are her clothing and she shall rejoice in time to come.

She opens her mouth with wisdom and in her tongue is the law of kindness.

She looks well to the ways of her household, and does not eat the bread of idleness.

Her children rise up and call her blessed; her husband also, and he praises her.

Charms may wane and beauty wither, but a woman who fears the Lord is to be praised.

Give her of the fruit of her hands, and let her own works praise her.

Excerpts from Proverbs 31

CHAPTER I **MATURITY** SHE IS
FAR MORE PRECIOUS
THAN JEWELS

"I have one great fear—that of growing old." This statement was made by a young man of twenty-five. With a few negative examples of old age in his environment, one could clearly understand his thinking. Yet he was not aware that he was confiding his dread to a woman nearly sixty. When we say "old," what do we mean? Dates are not an accurate measurement. One observer said that "old" was a person ten years older than you. Some women are physically old by thirty, while others maintain a good standard of health and appearance through their seventies. We have different rates of aging which do not correspond to years lived. Heredity is a determining factor plus the experiences of life.

FEAR OF CHANGE

If our surroundings are agreeable and we are comfortable, it is our nature to wish to remain static. We dislike going into new and unfamiliar situations. Yet it is this venturing forth that enriches our living. We experience many changes during our lives. Each time our fears subside after the first step into a new field. Our world enlarges as we emerge into a new era of our existence. We find we are capable of living in the new environment and we usually like it better than our former state.

There are several scenes and acts in a play. It moves from one situation to the next. How dull it would be to have one scene played over and over again, regardless of how pleasant the happening. Similarly, our lives move, and grow in the moving. What young child is not happy to give up his freedom and closeness to home for kindergarten after the first week's experience of learning with other children. When we placed our last doll on the shelf, there was a sadness, but not for long because of the school activities bursting on all sides. Later perhaps we feared marriage, the responsibilities and adjustments. We may have wit-

nessed closely an unhappy marriage. But
when the time came to solemnly venture
into this new era of life, again there was a
new dimension to our existence. Our children came and grew. One by one we had
the privilege of sharing their lives. Gradually they left for their wider horizons—beyond
that which we could give them. And now
is there any scene of our lives that we would
wish repeated, or are we ready to step into
the climax of our play? The mature woman
has gathered many interests along the way—
interests that reach back into her childhood.
She has dreamed many dreams that can
materialize in these unclaimed years. She
has a fortune in time. She has volumes of
experiences.

WHAT IS "OLD"?

In our present day, the span of life is increasing. During the Roman Empire 2,000
years ago, the average life expectancy was
23 years. Alexander the Great died at 33
and Napoleon at 52; both were old men.
In the United States in 1776, 35 years was
the average length of life. As late as 1900
it was 50 years. A child born in 1950 has
a life expectancy of 76 if it is a girl and 66 to

69 if a boy. Men attain greater age than women, but not as many reach old age.

There are various factors which determine longevity. Oliver Wendell Holmes said, "One of the best ways to insure a long life is to make a careful and wise selection of grandparents." Some fabrics are durable (burlap, denim, linens) and others are fragile (silks, chiffons), but even the strong material will deteriorate under stress and lack of care while the delicate can be preserved. This brings in the second factor which determines life-span—environment. This explains why some who have come from a long-lived family die young and those from the opposite type family enjoy a ripe old age.

The experiences of life can age or save a person. Physical infirmities enter in which give a false impression of one's competence, such as hearing or seeing. The number of years on the calendar is merely a guide and not a means of regimenting activity. An old tennis player might be a young grandmother. An old singer might be a young scientist. We mature gracefully when we can leave an area of interest and emerge into another with equal enthusiasm.

The desire to learn must be constantly fresh within us. The will to follow through and make the effort to achieve this learning is important. As we grow older we need a diversity of interests, not to the point of fragmentation but kept within the bounds of our physical abilities. Too much attachment to one thing limits our lives and our thinking, and if we should lose it there is nothing to soften the blow.

WE DEVELOP THROUGH THE YEARS

Numerical years are not the object of each life. Aging is not to be counted and endured but rather to be lived. The pursuits of earlier years have their time for disappearing, but they are still a part of the life which experienced them. That wisdom which has been the product of the learning and implemented knowledge of each life takes time to cultivate. There is no shortcut to maturity. It comes from being actively a part of each day—not withdrawing from life. It is giving your encouragement and good influence to projects of worth.

Maturing is a process of development from birth. It does not begin in the middle of life but is a constant emerging of the personality. It has been said that the woman of thirty is what the older woman at seventy will be—only more so. If she has a friendly outreach when she is younger, she will make friends and be a joy to her neighbors throughout her life. As an older woman she has more time, and will be able to take that home-baked pie in to the family whose mother is too busy to prepare such treats. She will remember birthdays. She will write letters—not expecting an answer but simply to express her good thoughts toward that person. The young woman who is neat in her appearance and her home will also be particular about cleanliness as she grows older.

Age does not gloss over faults; it emphasizes them. A woman at thirty who slides by on inaccuracy and poor planning may be excused with a laugh by her family and friends, but continuation on this plane will relegate her to the position of a muddled old lady who never gets things straight anyway. If she is tactless and rude, she will be worse as she ages. If she nags when younger, her habit will increase.

We are maturing every day. Each young woman needs to evaluate her habits and attitudes to recognize which way she is going. The advice to a young man about to choose a bride used to be, "Look at her mother and that is what your wife will be." This is not always true. Many young women with waspish mothers abhorred the example before them and resolved never to be that way. Sometimes those with gentle mothers chose to be the opposite, rebelling against all that represented goodness or discipline. Maturing is a personal growth, an individual accomplishment.

Fortunate is the little girl who is not the prettiest in her group, nor the owner of the largest doll, nor the one who has the best clothes. She will learn early the twinge of jealousy, but she will also learn to overcome it. She will learn the value of building good inner attitudes rather than using material possessions to achieve her desires. Her parents can help her in these first meetings with society by understanding her feelings and guiding her with Christian teachings.

Fortunate later is this little girl grown up who marries one who loves her; one who will praise her truthfully and criticize with understanding; one who will prick her to make a better effort, but one who knows that comparisons are invidious. This day-by-day living with others added to the inner capabilities, plus the heritage from our fore-bears, is represented in each person.

CULTIVATE DISCERNMENT OF OWN FAULTS AND ATTRIBUTES

Maturity is an achievement toward which we continuously strive. We do not reach it at a certain age, but perfect different attributes at different times. Some children display a remarkable quality of thoughtfulness in kindergarten. On the other hand, some women must use discipline most of their lives to be considerate of others. First we must recognize our lack and be teachable, with a will to correct or develop what is necessary.

There is nothing mysterious or uncontrollable about maturity. It can be a studied course of action after we evaluate our attitude toward ourselves and the world around us. Belief in self and respect for self is a necessity, but a "golden mean" must be established to avoid being self-centered. A woman may be capable, but unless she accepts responsibility, is dependable, and exerts herself to do things well, she has not achieved maturity. The mature woman will make mistakes, but will admit her error. Through her own vulnerability she will understand others' failures and be able to forgive and forget.

BE OPTIMISTIC AND ENCOURAGING

Optimism is a requirement in successful aging. When we express only our trials, we build fears and dreads in those who have not yet met that particular experience, thus destroying the interesting and joyful aspect of a new adventure. We need to studiously cultivate the habit of optimism and encouragement.

One of our greatest examples of this was in the life of Barnabas. It was Paul who gave the spectacular leadership, but he did not accomplish it alone. "Thus Joseph who was surnamed by the apostles Barnabas (which means, Son of encouragement), a Levite, a native of Cyprus, sold a field which belonged to him, and brought the money and laid it at the apostles' feet" (Acts 4:36, R.S.V.). He possessed the rare gift of seeing merit in others without being jealous or covetous. Paul needed this even-tempered, gracious man for the progress of Christianity. He needed encouragement.

One of the great attributes of an older person can be the spirit of lifting others to a sense of worth. Failures can weigh upon one like a huge debt, crushing out reason and even a will to survive. Unthinking complaints and criticism have an effect upon others. There is a desperate need for "Barnabases" in our society today.

Encouragement comes in assorted sizes and ways. It is not to be confused with flattery, the hollow lip service given without sincerity. It is given to support and motivate another who is in need of understanding. The spark of future accomplishment may be barely visible, but a word or listening face can make the difference between a glowing contribution or ashes.

Who needs encouragement? That secure young mother? Yes, she seems secure, but have you told her how well her children behaved the other day? She needs that recognition of her efforts. What about that confident young man who stood up and sang the solo? Nerves of steel? Well, perhaps— but it did require courage. If he continues with his talent, he will have to have some- one who will tell him he is appreciated. Did the minister say one thing that was helpful to you? Remember to tell him about it—not just a general "I enjoyed the sermon." If you miss him at the door write him a note and mail it. Have you any conception of the pressures on that carefree teen-ager? By your speech and example help him to maintain ethical standards of excellence. In this world of "grays" there are still black and white—a clear difference between right and wrong. Encourage him to achieve his goals without sacrificing conscience. He will need this small alarm system much longer than a passing grade in a current subject which he is studying.

PRAYER AND PARTICIPATION

These are the visible ways of support, but there is a vast area, unexplored by many—encouragement through prayer. One does not hear, one does not see, but one feels the freedom and lifting up when he is being sustained in prayer. The mature woman is aware of the power of the prayer of intercession and uses it for the sake of others. "More things are wrought by prayer than this world dreams of" (Tennyson, *Morte d'Arthur*).

One of the great dangers of old age is

withdrawal. At this period of our lives, the need to serve a family is not pressing, but to our own psyche it is vital that we keep in the stream of life. There must be something important enough that others will identify us with it. It is not enough to be financially secure, nor to know important people, nor to travel or be involved in recreation alone. There must be purpose. The French express it as *raison d'etre,* a reason for being.

The mature woman lives in a world of people and is aware that there must be an interaction between her and them. She must be outgoing and give of herself because of the concern she has for them. If she finds that this requires more effort than she desires to give, gradually her interest wanes in everything about her and she cannot be brought back to reality.

LOOK AT THE LARGER PICTURE

We learn to look at the larger picture and to choose our way with eternal values in mind. From the years of experience, we know what is important and will be able to wait for it. The child sees what he wants and must have immediately, whether it is a piece of candy or the moon. Understanding comes with self-discipline, and when our understanding is full grown, we "put away childish things."

Too long the negative aspects of personality have been predominant in our current literature. Society is obsessed with the "sick" side of life—insecurity, inferiority, frustration, guilt, ego protection. Although we must surely recognize and try to alleviate these ills, there needs to be an emphasis on the positive virtues of a normal, healthy personality. The old-fashioned qualities are still with us—loyalty, dignity, integrity, decency, but we seldom hear about them because they are less newsworthy.

Courage is a vital part of maturity. One must learn to make decisions after thoughtful, but not endless, consideration. Too often we deliberate a good idea into oblivion by too much weighing of the matter. We explore one possibility and then another, confusing and prolonging the problem until it assumes a proportion far greater than its original importance. Once more our experience and the inner development of ourselves should help us to move with "quiet confidence."

STABILITY IS IMPORTANT

The mature woman is stable. When she assumes a responsibility, it will be accomplished to the best of her ability. She will keep her word and not make rash promises. There is nothing more frustrating and wearing than a maze of unfinished tasks or a late performance. Alibis are never satisfactory even to the one who concocts them. It is difficult for a woman in later years to change from a flighty latecomer to a dependable member of society. She has developed an easy conscience about others' feelings, and if she is surrounded by the same people they have by this time relegated her to her proper place. One can change. Try this if you remotely resemble the unreliable type. When you accept an assignment, aim high and "go the second mile" in your preparation. Know the deadline and establish your own deadline a day or more earlier. Regardless of the request, make it creative to add interest for yourself if nothing more. Remember, anything worth doing is worth doing well—so work on it.

Very often it is difficult to stay with a project or a situation until it is finished. A child's interest span is quite short and we allow for it, but the adult who cannot stay with a particular work, one who tries this field and that, one who changes friends by whim is immature. Eventually nothing will interest her. Plutarch said, "Character is a long-standing habit." Becoming dependable is a habit practiced in every phase of our lives.

A few years ago, Mary Ethel Noland, a retired schoolteacher, wrote some "Do's and Don't's for the Mature Woman." She graciously assented to having them placed in this course. She is a cousin of the former President of the United States of America, Harry Truman.

"Stay where you are in the old home-town, in the old home. You have no roots in California or Florida.

"Don't look back. Don't visit the place where you worked—they may be polite but they are busy.

"Be satisfied with your income, since you have no way of increasing it.

"Pay bills promptly. Save energy by using mail.

"Buy clothes, etc., of good quality. Do not hesitate to enjoy pleasures and small luxuries that will not endanger your financial safety.

"Develop old skills and interests for which you now have time. Develop new skills and interests. Learn something new every day.

"Deepen old friendships. Keep up correspondence. Widen your acquaintances. Make new friends among different types of people. Be a good neighbor, a good church woman. Be friendly, but natural, with children and youth.

"Do not try to trade on your age. Don't expect privileges or favors because you are old.

"Do not depend on people or circumstances to make you happy—joy is within.

"Keep your perspective, your sense of values, your standards, your sense of humor. Laugh, but don't titter, nor snicker, nor cackle.

"Don't visit much. Go when invited and leave while they are still enjoying your visit.

"Don't be a telephone pest.

"Keep your manners above reproach—especially at table.

"When you live alone you have to be your own audience and censor. Avoid mannerisms.

"Grow a thick skin. Don't be touchy about your age (or anything else).

"Be fair to those you employ, but keep off the sucker list.

"Do gracious things for others. Let your gifts show thoughtfulness and taste rather than a large outlay of money which you cannot afford.

"Express that love and sympathy you feel.

"Enjoy small pleasures one at a time— the weather, the new moon, spring flowers, tomatoes from a neighbor's garden, frisky squirrels, a clean bed, a gentle rain.

"Keep your health by good dental care, advice of a good M.D. periodically, being daintily clean and presentable, walking when possible, eating sensibly (don't be too lazy to cook for yourself), doing some manual work every day, living in clean surroundings, forgetting self as much as possible.

"Have a regular schedule of time,

place, and occasions—not so rigid as to be driven by it, but have one.

"Let your life be free from clutter. Give away useful things to those who need them. Burn things that no longer are of value to anybody.

"Avoid sentimentality. Your griefs are your own. They have become part of you, but they will not be of interest to anyone else.

"Keep old letters and souvenirs that have historical value for the Historical Society. Burn the rest.

"Let your conversation be cheerful. Your ailments are not interesting.

"Face facts; be realistic—know your limitations.

"Be in command of yourself and the situation.

"Make the most of your religion; claim its promises; enjoy its privileges; assume its responsibilities.

"Justify your existence.

"Keep striving for self-mastery.

"Always remember love is the greatest thing in the world."

As a woman matures, she gains many

credits to her name whether her career is business, professional, or homemaking. Her image is formed by what she thinks, says, and does. The final masterpiece is a composite of her reactions to life and her contributions to family and society. She stands alone on what she has done with her physical, mental, and spiritual inheritance in this world.

CHAPTER 2 **APPEARANCE** STRENGTH AND DIGNITY ARE HER CLOTHING

Every woman wishes to be beautiful. It is a worthwhile objective when clearly understood, but too many women are satisfied with partial truth concerning beauty, leaving wide gaps in the total picture. The beautiful woman is a composite of properties which satisfy the ear, the eye, the intellect, and the spirit. The Roman school described beauty as "multitude in unity."

Two thousand years ago, timeless advice was given to women: "Your beauty should reside, not in outward adornment—the braiding of the hair, or jewelry, or dress—but in the inmost center of your being" (I Peter 3:4, N.E.B.).

According to Peter, a Christian woman is known by her inner beauty of character rather than by ornamentation. This is the imperishable part of us, the divine side that will live and grow. The wise woman knows that her spirit reflects in her body—her eyes, her mouth, the way she walks. As she matures, she expresses her life more clearly, gradually putting aside the insecurities and small foibles to make way for her true self. Her appearance is always important to her, but wisdom places the emphasis properly.

Maturity has a beauty all its own. It has the benefit of the preceding years' experiences—the enrichment of spirit, poise, understanding. An older woman has had time to develop good taste in many fields. By listening to the works of great composers, she acquires appreciation for music. By reading the classics and other good literature, she has an appreciation for books. Through the years she has accumulated insight into the good things of life. These cannot be taken away. They are reflected in all she says or does and in the choices she makes.

The mature woman is well groomed for two reasons: (1) It helps her own self-respect, and (2) she has a regard for those around her. It is not false pride when we keep our house in order. A family living in love and contentment in a home with dirty windows and a careless yard would have difficulty convincing their neighbors of their worth in the community. A woman of good intent but lacking cleanliness and neatness would meet obstacles also. A first impression is usually gained visually. No matter where you go someone will see you and notice how you look. We need to make ourselves as beautiful as possible.

THE YOUTHFUL IMAGE

In our present society there has been a tremendous accent on youth—particularly youthful women. Men can mature gracefully into their seventies, but women must remain at thirty in appearance. Ridiculous, yes, but that is our image for today and it is a challenge. We must remember, however, that trying to be beautiful is like trying to be happy; we lose it if we lack wisdom in our search. It comes from within and reflects in our attitude.

Do not worry about the passing years. Fear of aging only hastens it. The sorriest sight is a woman desperately clinging to youth and pretending to be a generation younger—mimicking the speech, the dress, the makeup of the teen-ager. Robert Burns could have had such a person in mind when he wrote,

Oh wad some power the giftie gie us
To see oursels as ithers see us:
It wad frae mony a blunder free us,
   An' foolish notion:
What airs in dress an' gait wad lea'e us,
   An' ev'n devotion!

This does not mean we should ignore current style. We are still in the world, but we must adapt the trends to our age and figure. We can develop imagination and visualize what is appropriate for us, thus keeping us in the present without sacrificing our dignity.

HEALTH IS IMPORTANT

Maturity is not the beginning of uselessness but rather a broadening of achievement. At this age there is a need for accurate information regarding our physical well-being. We should know and understand the basic facts of our body function. The enlightened woman knows what might happen, but she is not worrying needlessly over things that will not happen. The woman who has carefully observed the rules of good health through proper balance of nutrition, exercise, and rest begins to receive the benefits of her early training.

We cannot look well if we do not feel well. We start aging when we are born, but we do not all age the same way. One can have young hands but an old heart, or strong arms but feeble legs. Our future years depend largely on the care and wisdom we use now. Many diseases start unnoticed in middle life—diabetes, cancer, heart disease. They are insidious in that they give no outer sign. Only a doctor can recognize them and in many cases either cure or bring them under control. A woman in her middle years should have a medical checkup at least once a year or every six months if possible. This is a worthwhile investment toward later life.

Most women are afraid of being categorized as hypochondriacs, so they continue through the latter part of their lives just bearing an ache or pain that could be healed. They excuse their poor health with phrases like these: "I guess it's old age creeping up" or "I'll have to learn to live with it" or "What I don't know won't hurt me." With medical knowledge at its present level, it is not intelligent to suffer in silence. Remarkable discoveries are being made daily—new attacks on old diseases. Many times a life has a new beginning with simple surgery or a few pills. Seek medical guidance early with any unusual symptoms and follow instructions. If medicine is prescribed, take it when you should. If a rest period or exercise is needed, follow the advice. If diet is recommended, enjoy what you can have rather than bemoaning what you cannot have. Do not hesitate to ask your doctor questions. If you are prone to forget, write them out. We owe it not only to ourselves but to those who may have to care for us to keep our health as long as possible.

Life itself is a blessing and aging is a part of life, a part of the larger plan of existence. There is a normal body slowdown. Certain physiological changes occur. The loss of elasticity of the lens of the eyes begins at about the age of ten and is completed before the age of sixty. Acuteness of taste begins to decline at fifty and that of smell at sixty. Hearing begins to fail at twenty.

When we look for a telephone number, we may have to hold the book at arm's length. We used to wonder about grandmother "feeling draughts" in the room or in the car when every place seemed the same temperature to us. Now we know. When these small annoyances begin to appear, we are no longer relegated to a corner.

How thankful we are for the props that keep us a part of society—eyeglasses, hearing aids, dentures, and any other aid we may need. It is better to admit the handicap, then do something about it. Unfortunately, some older persons have the "ostrich attitude" of putting their heads in the sand—hoping they won't be noticed or maybe the affliction will pass. Thus they become irritable because they are uncomfortable. Helpful devices such as good dentures or a hearing aid may seem expensive, but if they will help us take better care of ourselves, they are not extravagant but a wise investment. It requires patience to become accustomed to false teeth, hearing aids, and bifocals, but in order to remain a part of the world in which we live it is important to strengthen or replace that worn part of the body, if possible.

NUTRITION

A woman who has been conditioned and educated to proper nutrition throughout her life has a rare asset to support her older years. At twenty-five, scientists tell us, the body is in its prime. Development stops and we need less food every year, but a healthful balance must continue. A study was made by food scientists at several midwest agricultural experiment stations. They discovered that women between 40 and 59 had diets 9 percent below par in protein; between 60 and 69 they had 18 percent below; between 70 and 79 they had 12 percent below. Even though body growth is completed, we still need protein for repair and upkeep of body tissues. These foods are important: milk, cheese, eggs, meats, poultry, and fish.

A woman still needs sufficient calories to maintain energy and normal weight. There are many reliable books and pamphlets available concerning nutrition. Rapid reducing and freak diets accomplish one thing—a rapid weight loss—but this is not the answer. There must be a reeducation to the right eating habits, a candid evaluation of the problems involved, and intelligent will to persevere. Avoid the food faddists.

In later years there may be problems which decrease the enjoyment of eating. If there is a need for dental work, do not neglect these repairs. If chewing is difficult, do not resort to tea and toast or the result will be malnutrition. Meat can be ground and vegetables mashed or chopped. There are varieties in baby food and they are nutritious, but they may need seasoning.

Poor eating habits in later years are many times psychological. If the family has diminished to two or possibly one, plan ahead just as you did when the children were growing. A meal thrown together at the last minute usually tastes that way. Allow time for an oven dinner rather than a hurried sandwich. Eat fairly regular meals, each one properly served. Be careful to buy only that amount which you can easily use. The large economy size is not the least expensive if it grows stale or spoils. Be adventurous with new recipes and have a ready file. By now you are quite an expert in your judgment of what tastes good by simply scanning the ingredients.

We are more likely to eat slowly and enjoy our meals if the surroundings are pleasant. Let's not get into the habit of eating all our meals in the kitchen just because the family is no longer with us. Mats can be placed on individual trays and carried to a table or chair by a window or out on the porch or patio. If there are two, remember candlelight is very flattering. If alone, take the companionship of a book or radio or TV, but be selective. This can be a growing time.

Sometimes an appetite needs to be coaxed. A short walk or light exercise is helpful, but not to the point of exhaustion. Make the food interesting with a different flavor. Include a crispy food to contrast with the soft. Be conscious of color—white mashed potatoes with white cauliflower and white fish on a white plate would have a pallid taste regardless of seasoning. Harmonize the centerpiece, tablecloth, dishes, and food. Enjoy the good china at least once a week. Our daughters would much rather we used it; they may not even care for our pattern. Some of the pieces will be broken, but the tragedy is to see beauty covered up in a closet and the one to whom it was given saving it for someone else. So discard the chipped plates and cheese glasses and improve your appetite.

As we grow older, it becomes a greater task to prepare and manage large dinners and parties, but this does not close all doors to entertainment. We can still invite someone in occasionally for a chat and light refreshments. If we make an effort to be informed and interesting, our invitations will be welcome. We do not have to entertain someone our own age. Children are often delighted to have special attention. The mature woman can speak with any generation.

SLEEPING

Proper rest is a necessity for good appearance. Fatigue lines and strain are caused by either physical or psychological problems. Possibly a simple correction in our daily living may be enough, or it may go much deeper. It is not the quantity nor regularity of sleep that we have, for we all differ in our requirements. It does need to be a quality that will recondition us. Shakespeare decribes it as "Sweet sleep, sleep that knits up the ravelled sleeve of care."

A good bed is essential. Choose it with you own comfort in mind (even the three bears were selective). Electric blankets and new weaves have taken the place of heavy quilts for warmth. The weight of improper bedclothing can make us tired. Correct room temperatures vary with individuals. The more rugged type feels better with the snow blowing into the room, while another sets her thermostat at 75. As one grows older, a pillow is an important part of good rest. Comfortable nightclothes can induce sleep. Uncomfortable nightclothes can retard sleep. And do let that nightclothing be attractive. Do not save all those nighties for traveling or a quick trip to the hospital. Wear them and enjoy them.

Fatigue lines also are etched on our faces when we go beyond our strength. No two persons are alike—not even identical twins. A physical challenge to one may be a simple task to another. There are German shepherd dogs and Chihuahuas with everything in between. People are that way too. By the time we are forty, we should have a good idea of how much we can stand and how to work around our weaknesses.

Eyestrain also causes fatigue. When did you last have an examination by an ophthalmologist? A simple thing like poor lighting can be wearing.

EXERCISE

We need exercise all our lives. The amount and kind depend largely upon our habits and the training we have had in our earlier years. Age affects our physical exercise very little if it has become a part of our daily routine. This has been proven by professional swimmers, dancers, and actresses whose careers depend upon keeping physically fit. Dame Margot Fonteyn, a woman in her fifties, is still giving magnificent performances in one of the most strenuous artistic fields—ballet. In countries where walking, mountain climbing, skating, skiing, or swimming are a part of everyday life, older persons continue to be active in these areas, but they choose their own pace. It is wise to select sports that are not as competitive, thus avoiding strenuous exertion. Those living in cities tend to become more sedentary, but there is always the opportunity to walk. We miss this because our minds have become accustomed to planning our goings and comings on the split second, thus necessitating use of a car.

Gardening provides pleasure and exercise with bending and lifting. If our knees will no longer allow stooping, a cushion to kneel upon will aid. Most of us step into our yard and spot a weed, then we are off, pulling one here and another and another. Just a hint: be sure to keep a pair of old gloves handy.

HANDS

A mature woman's hands were not meant to be like a young girl's. The skin ages and sometimes the joints become enlarged, but the beauty of older hands comes from use and caring for others. This does not mean they should be neglected. Daily care is essential throughout the years. Nails should be well groomed and this can be done while resting or listening. The selection of polish should be in lighter tones to harmonize with the hand. An occasional gesture is interesting, but continuous fluttering indicates nervousness and a lack of vocabulary. In ordinary conversation we should be able to express thoughts and emotions by choice of words, tone of voice, or expression of eyes. Hands can be a great beauty asset.

GRACE

A man made this observation, "Grace is one of the neglected beauty factors of the Western world. There is a flow to the way a tranquil woman walks and sits and looks at you."

Beauty in motion is an important part of our appearance. Physical handicaps in later years such as arthritis rob some of the freedom of movement of youth. But the main cause of awkward mannerisms lies not in physical disability but rather in carelessly practicing bad habits until they are a part of us. Our posture while sitting and walking becomes automatic—and it might as well be good.

Have you observed your walk lately as you passed by a mirror or a store window? Do you waddle? Do you shamble? Do you lead with your head? Do your toes go in or go out? Back up against a wall and line yourself up, then walk forward. There should be a free swing forward at the hips, knees, and ankles. Lift the entire foot off the floor and step down on the whole foot. The legs should move close enough to each other so that the knees graze in passing. There should be only one line of footprints behind you. This can be practiced on a chalkline or a seam in a carpet. It will take time to correct an awkward walk, but it will make a difference. Give thought to how you walk and develop habits that automatically control your movements whether serving family dinner or walking across a platform.

It may seem unimportant to be concerned about sitting, but this also reveals a picture either lovely or ugly. An ordinary chair should not present any problems to the average woman. Simply stand with one leg just touching the front of it and the other foot slightly ahead to gain balance. Lower yourself lightly with back and head erect. Be sure to cross your legs at the ankle instead of the knee. Either sitting or standing, do not let your knees spread apart. We mentioned "ordinary chairs," but getting into and out of automobiles is an individual problem. In spite of our super inventions, we find ourselves waving arms and legs like beetles on their backs trying to get a footing. Everything works against us, even to the short sheaths. Plan your entrance and egress as best you can, without sacrificing too much dignity.

ACCENTUATE THE POSITIVE

How we look as we grow older is important to us and those around us. First, we must discover our good points and accent them. This is the advice of a woman crippled with rheumatoid arthritis. She had very little left of beauty of appearance, but her face and head were attractive. She concentrated on facial exercises when she had the opportunity. She had plenty of rest. For her makeup she selected carefully the right shades for her. Her hair had turned white so she put aside the black dresses and wore cheerful colors which emphasized her lovely face and eyes. She worked diligently with her hands even though they were obviously rheumatic. Her nails were carefully groomed and polished. She accepted the fact that her body was out of line and wore dresses with full or pleated skirts. These things were not simple for her to do because of physical limitations and pain, but she realized the importance of being scrupulously groomed. It helped her in her other worthwhile activities.

SMILE

Facial expressions invite or repel. Many faces in repose are the opposite to what lies beneath. It is when they become animated that they can be beautiful. A smile does more for the countenance than any cosmetic. It can change hostile attitudes of other people. Since any smile automatically exposes your teeth, regular care must be given them to give you confidence. But above all, your smile must originate from within; otherwise it will mean nothing. The eyes must help to express it as well as the lips—and don't worry about the facial lines it might cause. A wise woman said, "So long as a woman has twinkles in her eyes, no man notices whether she has wrinkles under them."

GROOMING

It takes planning to be well groomed. True, accidents happen to the most fastidious at times, but many unpleasant surprises can be avoided. The woman who continuously appears with food spots on her clothing, or dog hairs on her skirt, or runs in her hosiery, or slip showing needs a full-length mirror in a well lighted room and a little time for inspection. Makeup should be applied in a good light so that natural beauty can be delicately accentuated; avoid makeup which produces a harsh clown mask.

For some reason, it does take us longer to "get ready" to go out than when we were younger. We need to allow for this and plan to sit in a chair for at least five minutes before the appointed time instead of scurrying out the door and buttoning on the way. A well-groomed woman may move swiftly, but she does not give the impression of being hurried or scattered. She is confident in her appearance.

OUR IMAGE

The body we possess is a gift to us and should be regarded as such. We did not earn it, but it was placed in our care to serve us during our probation period on earth. It has been called a "vessel" in biblical language, and rightly so, for it carries the precious contents of our whole person. A woman is a many-faceted creature. Like the raindrop in the sun when light is reflected and refracted showing the inner beauty of the spectrum, so her life is transformed when the pure light of Christ shines through her.

In ancient America, Alma asked this question of the people, "Have ye received his image in your countenances?" (Alma 3:28). The qualities of life represented by Christ can become so ingrained upon a soul that they are visible—"love, joy, peace, patience, kindness, goodness, faithfulness, gentleness, self-control; against such there is no law" (Galatians 5:22-23, R.S.V.).

The image we bear is important.

CHAPTER 3 **MIND** SHE OPENETH
HER MOUTH
WITH WISDOM

One of the greatest neces-
sities of a full life is a sense of wonder,
coupled with a healthy curiosity about the
world in which we live and the people with
whom we live. If these childlike attributes
are dulled, we are no longer a part of a
moving, growing creation.

NO NEW THING

The pessimistic preacher in Ecclesiastes
tells us, "There is no new thing under the
sun." According to his understanding and
background, there was probably very little
change in his surroundings during his lifetime. Today with our rapid transportation
and immediate communication, we live in
the opposite type of world, but we too can
become jaded and miss the impact of God's
signature on our beings. As we grow older,
although we have seen and heard many

things, we cannot allow wonder to escape our nature. There may be "no new thing" but there are new interpretations continuously appearing.

"We cease to wonder at what we understand" (Samuel Johnson). When we have learned every facet of a problem it no longer holds a mystery to be solved. But in the scope of our existence, there is so much yet to be understood that we cannot possibly afford to lose our sense of wonder.

> The world is so full of a number of things
> I'm sure we should all be as happy as kings.
> —ROBERT LOUIS STEVENSON

THE CHILD

Jesus said, "Whosoever shall not receive the kingdom of God as a little child, he shall not enter therein" (Mark 10:15, K.J.V.).

There are many characteristics of childhood which gradually become overlaid with civilization unless care is taken to preserve or exercise characteristics of worth. The child reminds us of dependence, outgoing love, honesty, and many other virtues, but probably the most universal trait is his sense of wonder—wonder of people, wonder of nature, wonder of machines, wonder of everything around him.

Walk with a child and look through his eyes. See that amazing caterpillar. Watch that ant carrying something twice its size. Observe the construction of that dandelion. What makes those particles glisten in that rough stone? We soon learn how "uncommon" our world is as we observe and think with the poet:

Flower in the crannied wall,
I pluck you out of the crannies,
I hold you here, root and all, in my hand,
Little flower—but if I could understand
What you are, root and all, and all in all,
I should know what God and man is.
—ALFRED LORD TENNYSON

Watch a baby who is discovering his hand for the first time. Carefully he moves his fingers, then brings them closer to his eyes for a better view. He opens and closes his fist, touches it with his other hand, totally engrossed. Have you observed your hand lately?

THE PSALMISTS

The psalmists were sensitive to the wonders of God and spoke in praise and thanksgiving. While other Old Testament scriptures deal with law and ritual, the Psalms bring another side of the Hebrew faith—a deeper value of the spiritual.

Psalm 19:1—"The heavens declare the glory of God; and the firmament showeth his handiwork."

Psalm 8:3—"When I consider thy heavens, the work of thy fingers, the moon and the stars, which thou hast ordained; what is man, that thou art mindful of him? and the son of man, that thou visitest him?"

Psalm 136, selections—"Give thanks unto the Lord . . . To him who alone doeth great wonders . . . To him that by wisdom made the heavens . . . To him that stretched out the earth above the waters . . . To him that made great lights . . . The sun to rule by day . . . The moon and stars to rule by night."

Psalm 139:14—"I will praise thee; for I am fearfully and wonderfully made; marvellous are thy works; and that my soul knoweth right well."

EXERCISE SENSES

God gave us our senses and a world in which to use them. If they are neglected, they will deteriorate, just as any other physical part of us does when we do not exercise it. Some years ago in a course of music a test was given to evaluate the students' sense of hearing. It was on a recording. Two different tones were sounded and we wrote on the paper whether they were "high - low" or "low - high." At the beginning they were a step apart and easily discernible. Gradually the pitches moved closer until to most of the group there was no difference. One girl continued to write, and when the test was completed she had missed only one. The reason for her accurate hearing came from years of playing the harp and keeping her instrument in tune. She had listened for the slightest variance of pitch from the time she was a child. This continuous exercise of her sense of hearing produced an accuracy which far exceeded that of the average person.

There are familiar sounds all around us which we hear subconsciously. It would be a disturbing existence if every sound were registered upon our minds. But who can ignore the song of the cardinal on a spring morning—or the tree frogs on a warm summer night?

Our sense of sight or observation should

increase as our experience grows. We have many objects and scenes in our memory to which we can relate the present. Yet, unless we see intelligently, many wondrous things will pass our vision unnoticed, and we will rob ourselves of life's pleasures through lack of attention. Do you view a rainbow with indifference or as the poet sees it?

> My heart leaps up when I behold
> A rainbow in the sky:
> So was it when my life began;
> So is it now I am a man;
> So be it when I shall grow old,
> Or let me die!
>
> —WORDSWORTH

We need to keep this innate ability to wonder. We must be curious about our surroundings, about people, about ideas. This is the brink of learning. Before we pursue knowledge, we first wonder. A person who through the years finds no quickening within him through sight or sound or thought has lost life itself. Man was created to have joy and the joy of discovery is primary.

CHANGES

As we move through life we change both physically and mentally. Our thought processes are different as we age. The older mind is no better nor worse, for in some areas we lose and in others we gain. Our reactions become slower, but our judgment increases. A young person will take risks and depend upon his reflexes, but the older person will be more careful and avoid the situation. Our memory is less efficient, but our reasoning power is better. Scholastically speaking it may require much more effort for an older mind to memorize—for part of our learning is by rote. But if we can relate it to what we know and reason the answer, it may take longer but it will remain. Creative imagination is not limited to the early years. In fact, if it is exercised it will increase. It is true that many persons reach their greatest heights in their youth or middle years, but many more develop continuously. This occurs when there are many interests and a variety of experiences.

We retain our abilities through continuous discipline. The more we exercise the thought processes, the greater our capacity becomes. We have read of the remarkable intelligence of men like Albert Schweitzer, Winston Churchill, and Thomas Edison. Their interests spanned many fields.

Their minds were indefatigable, constantly gathering new things, ever pushing aside the limiting walls.

AGING AND DEFECTIVE CELLS

In an article by Howard Curtis, "What Science Knows About Aging," we read:

"When we critically examine an older person we can see the consequences of these defective cells. Blood vessels which carry nutrients to all parts of the body have cells in the vessel walls which go to pieces and cannot repair themselves. Thus a small volume of tissue is deficient in nutrients and performs poorly. This is true for all parts of the body. There are special cells in the hair follicles responsible for the color of the hair, and as they go bad the hair becomes colorless. Muscle cells tend to go bad, and coupled with the poor blood vessels, cause muscular weakness. The cells of the skin die, leaving behind a residue called collagen, which gradually shrinks and causes the wringled skin of old age.

"But in the midst of this rather gloomy picture there is a bright spot. The brain cells seem exceptionally stable, and whereas we lose a few as we grow older, there seems to be such an excess that thought processes can continue with very little decrement until late in life. It is only necessary to keep the mind active to keep it working well."

MEMORY

Older persons remember incidents which occurred many years ago easier than the immediate past. The reason for this is that impressions gained in youth are cut deeper in the memory pattern. As we grow older certain things become less important to us. We have learned so many names, addresses, and telephone numbers over fifty to eighty years that they are no longer prominent in our thinking. But we probably will never forget the name of the boy who invited us to our first party. Perhaps our greatest impairment to memory is our lack of attention. So many habits have been established through repetition that we do not think.

For example: Consider the times you have walked to the refrigerator while preparing a dinner, opened the door, and stood there not being able to recall why you were there. Then you closed the door, went back to where you were, and in a few moments you knew what you wanted from the refrigerator. After a few years of caring for a family, a woman can prepare a complete breakfast without consciously being aware of what she is doing. There will be memory lapses occasionally in later years. When they occur, do not think you are losing your mind. You are thinking of something else. Samuel Johnson said, "The true art of memory is the art of attention."

In this day of scheduling, most women use notebooks or calendars to remember the many events and duties which require their time. It is better to write it down than to clutter your mind.

Tie a string with a pencil to the telephone and keep a pad of paper handy in case an important message comes in.

If dates are important to you, keep a loose-leaf calendar by your bed. Each night turn it to the next day. You will know when you awaken what day it is (if this bothers you).

Do not panic if you happen to forget. Your memory is not really damaged. Remember—the teen-ager forgets some very important things too and no one points a finger at his mind.

A doctor recommends self-improvement as an aid to memory. We need new things to occupy our minds, for as our years increase there will be dull times, periods of apprehension, gloom, and fear. If we dwell on the negative, it affects our outlook and ultimately our minds and bodies.

CONTINUE LEARNING

We have read of the under-achiever, the child who has the ability to learn plus the environment to nurture his intelligence but who lacks the desire. This is a critical problem in youth. Yet we have many more under-achievers in our older group. There are too many women of intelligence whose families are grown who have ceased learning. Now is the time to complete those unfinished dreams that were interrupted twenty years ago. Although much has happened in that time, you probably have another twenty years to accomplish this. Grandmothers are back in college and graduating with honors. Perhaps you do not live near a school. All state universities have correspondence courses which are within your ability to understand. No day should end without some new thing learned. No year should pass without a period of disciplined achievement.

The saying was "You can't teach an old dog new tricks," but it has changed to "You can teach him any tricks he really wants to learn" (Dr. Edward Stieglitz). Then, too, there are some tricks which lie only within the capability of an "old dog." Whether you decide to pursue the studies with which you are familiar or go into an entirely new field, it is always well to have a plan—some short-time goals and longtime goals. "Dabbling" is good up to a point but the disciplines of achieving an objective carry satisfaction.

There are different ways of using the mind. If we add a new fact to what we already know, no matter how small, we have started thought processes. When we carefully reason through two sides of a question and make a decision, we are thinking. Finding a new way to do something better requires thought.

Teaching is also a learning process. Although the subject has been thoroughly studied, interaction with a student presents other areas not thought of before. Having the correct answers may be knowledge, but imagination and insight are required to enlarge this knowledge into wisdom.

ADULT EDUCATION

Many experiments have been made in adult education. Teachers have found that older students are better motivated in their interest to learn. They also bring knowledge and experience gathered through the years which greatly enrich the class.

Two colleges in the east developed a program to appeal to persons over sixty. They agreed to admit them as auditors, tuition free, provided there was room in the particular class chosen. Entrance exams were waived, but an application and interview were required for screening. The classes were publicized in the local newspaper giving the course content and the goals of the program. In order to test the interest, the applicant had to call to request a form, complete it, and return it to the college office. The form included a list of fifteen topics from which to choose six. Ninety percent qualified, making a student body of over one hundred. Thirty-one percent held college degrees, 24 percent had attended college, and 25 percent were high school graduates.

The one subject the college avoided was "problems of aging." It is well to know the pitfalls of growing older, but they are being stressed too much. Older persons do not mind hearing about areas in their lives that need improving, but they are also interested in oceanography, languages, geology, and many other fields.

The older student is more discriminating. The teacher must be interesting as well as learned, but he cannot talk down to the class. Older students are courteous but cannot be regimented. By this time vocabulary and word usage is at its peak so that the student can express himself better then ever before.

NEW DISCOVERIES

A new scientific era is opening. Doctors are investigating the mysterious labyrinths of the mind to understand how this complex organ functions. They are discovering drugs to influence the way it operates. In an experiment, a drug has been proven effectual in helping children read by blocking out distracting noises and enabling the child to concentrate.

A neurobiologist has discovered that learning causes an increase in the production of a certain chemical in the brain cells. These cells can be transferred from one creature to another. We may soon be able to learn much faster through transplants. "Memory" pills before examinations are being tried by college students even now.

With the advent of the marvels of mind control there will be social and moral problems, for every great gift of mankind reopens the "Pandora box." The new vistas before those who are older are significant. How we use these new discoveries is most important.

INSOMNIA

Sleeplessness is not unusual as we grow older. Much of our best thinking is accomplished in the middle of the night. Always keep a notebook on the night table so that ideas worth remembering can be written down. Then we can feel secure in knowing that they will not be lost.

This is an ideal time for concentrated study when all the rest of the world is asleep. However, if your aim is to sleep, just keep a book available which is not too exciting and read until you become drowsy.

This is a very good time to offer specific prayers for persons you know or know about.

DISCERNMENT

As we study, our capacity to discern increases. It becomes second nature for us to choose what is best in the field we know. We become more selective. A woman who studies good literature, who subscribes to thoughtful periodicals, who reads to improve her thinking and not entirely for amusement will never be satisfied with "husks." Her comprehension of the best will not allow her to waste time on the cheap and the sensational.

Good music is not always difficult music any more than good literature consists only of four or five syllable words. Discrimination beween best and mediocre is the result of a learning process whether by formal training or by being "caught." After comprehension of beauty and perfection in music come into a life, a primitive beat and monotonous melody can no longer hold interest.

Discernment is a vital need in maturation. What we choose to quicken our intelligence and satisfy our spirit should be on a level that can grow and inspire. The farsighted woman will gather as much knowledge as possible as she travels toward old age.

Obviously, if we are to improve our taste, we must apply our minds to familiarizing ourselves with painting, sculpture, literature, music, and design that are recognized as the best.

MANY CHOICES OF STUDY

The fields of study are limitless. With a possible twenty years ahead of us we could become quite proficient in many subjects. We are commanded to study and to learn. We are urged to become knowledgeable, to fulfill our stewardship.

In Doctrine and Covenants 85:21, the following areas are mentioned:

"the doctrine of the kingdom"—theology

"things in heaven"—astronomy, meteorology, the space age

"things in earth"—agriculture, botany, ocean-ography

"things under the earth"—geology, mining

"things which have been"—history

"things which are"—current events

"things which must shortly come to pass"—prophecy

"things which are at home"—sociology, politics, racial problems, labor disputes

"things which are abroad"—travel, world affairs

"the wars and perplexities of nations"—international law, international peace

"countries and kingdoms"—geography, language, customs, industry

With all our ability to learn and to retain we still must have the desire within. There has to be background in a life and this is the reason for study. Education frees a person for better service. If the mind is well furnished we need never worry about a place to use it.

"Get thy spindle and thy distaff ready and the Lord will send thee flax."

CHAPTER 4 **SERENITY** IN HER TONGUE
IS THE LAW
OF KINDNESS

Serenity comes from within. A brief scanning of our acquaintances proves this. It is possible for a woman with beautiful surroundings, a loving family, mental capabilities, physical attractiveness, and any other advantage never to experience the inner peace so important to the mature woman. Happiness lies not so much in what you have as in how you appreciate what you have. It cannot be bought. It cannot be inherited. It is cultivated and nurtured a bit at a time through discipline, intelligence, and a knowledge that "all things work together for good to them that love God" (Romans 8:28). The serene woman is at peace with herself and the world about her—not by withdrawal but by warm human relationships and a life of activity and service.

There is a children's story which tells of

a king who offered a prize to the artist who could best depict "peace." Many paintings appeared—a still blue lake edged with pine, a summer sky, a restful sunset, and others. Each brought an influence of quiet. The people were astounded when the king chose a picture of a turbulent waterfall lurching over a jagged precipice. The sky was lowering and lightning discharged in sharp contrast. This all seemed the opposite of the king's request until they looked more closely. Behind the waterfall a weathered bush grew. In the bush sat a mother bird on her nest— perfect peace. This is serenity, the ability to be inwardly secure regardless of the buffeting of life around you.

Boris Pasternak, Nobel Prize winner, said,

"In this era of world wars, in this atomic age, values have changed. We have learned that we are the guests of existence, travelers between two stations. We must discover security within ourselves. During our short span of life we must find our own insights into our relationship with the existence in which we participate so briefly. Otherwise, we cannot live. This means, as I see it, a departure from the materialistic view of the twentieth century. It means a re-awakening of the spiritual world, of our inner life—of religion. I do not mean religion as a dogma or as a church, but as a vital feeling."

Isaiah knew the problems of the world, for he saw his people struggle with the ways of the Egyptians. He witnessed their compromises and alliances which were keeping Israel unsteady. He understood that the only solution to their dilemma, the only way they could be safe, was to return to their God and to follow His way, thus receiving the quietness of mind and the confidence to move forward. He said, "In returning and rest shall ye be saved; in quietness and in confidence shall be your strength" (Isaiah 30:15).

Our serenity will be a "will o' the wisp" many times. Incidents will occur to make us temporarily lose it. We will be chagrined to see how little is required to make it slip from our fingers. But as we increase in wisdom and understanding of our whole selves, we will know better how to cope with things that disconcert us. Peace of mind can be an abiding presence if we "practice the presence of God."

Analyze the day that is before you. A young navigator in World War II told of this experience. Each morning at dawn he went to the bridge of the ship to take a bearing and plot the course for the day. Yesterday's bearing was not accurate for the day ahead. Changes had to be made. Similarly, we face our new day and plan our course. Certain things are sure. The day may bring nothing more difficult than a succession of little tasks. We will not have to work continuously even though the day is long, crowded, and tense. There will be moments to catch our breath and let down—time to stop and rest.

Close the door of the mind to at least some anxieties and regrets. They will creep in but do not let them stay. One woman expressed a daily philosophy in the following:

This is the day the Lord has made.
He presented it, clean and lovely,
As the night birds fluttered home
And the ecstasy of sunrise
Filled the eastern sky.
It is His gift,
And I will use it thankfully;
Filling each small second

With buoyant purpose,
  tingling awareness,
    triumphant praise.

This is the day the Lord has made.
I will rejoice and be glad in it.

POISE

Poise is valuable in every age but particularly desirable in the older woman. By
this time her experiences should have given
her assurance in most situations. She needs
to believe in herself.

Many shy young women develop into confident matrons through self-discipline. The
secret is to focus interest on other people.
When we give something of ourselves to
someone—our ideas or better still, our attention—we forget our timidity. If we are in a
large group we should concentrate upon one
person at a time instead of vaguely trying to
see everyone at once.

An interesting observation was made of a
young speaker before a large audience. As
she began, her shoulders were bent as if
she were cold, her face was visibly tense, her
voice wavered slightly. As she progressed
in her subject, she became involved in what

she was saying. Her body straightened, her face became young and lovely, and her voice was vibrant. She was transformed because she let go of herself and lost the burden of senseless fear that covered her in the beginning.

Paul said, "For God hath not given us the spirit of fear; but of power, and of love, and of a sound mind."

Fear can destroy our efforts, but faith can magnify them. The woman of poise makes preparation in every way that she is able, then puts her trust in God.

GRACIOUSNESS

We sing "Gracious Spirit, dwell with me, I myself would gracious be."

This is said simply yet reaches the heart of graciousness. It is the Spirit of God dwelling within us that makes us forget ourselves and consider others. It is not a veneer because that would wear away under stress, but it is solidly built from the inside.

Often timid people are proud people. They become self-conscious and try to be impressive which leads them into saying and doing things which are opposite to what they intended. This occurs more often in youth than in older women, but even with long experience one can lose her grace with a rude "public servant" or one who slyly takes her parking space.

Warm manners are the natural outcome of graciousness. They are a universal aid to govern us when we might otherwise be thoughtless of others. Many women have never read page one of a book of etiquette, but their knowledge of the right thing to say or do at the right time is innate. A certain amount of knowledge regarding social custom is desirable, but the spirit behind it is most important. What is correct in the United States may be quite offensive in India and vice versa. Christ never made rules in a material sense—they would have been obsolete by now—but his rules of conduct in a spiritual sense are everlasting.

Gracious receiving is a problem for some people whether it is a gift, a favor, a compliment, or a courtesy. We have reached the age when young people are doing things for us—and how difficult it is sometimes for us to accept their help gracefully. When a younger person offers a chair or holds a door open, accept with thanks instead of an embarrassed "Don't bother about me" attitude. Above all never appear surprised at his thoughtfulness. We have been serving youth for many years—pushing their chairs in, shoving them ahead of us through doors and into cars. The transition is not easy, but it is necessary. A young person "feels good" when he does something for someone. He should not be robbed of this appreciation.

Shakespeare said, "When our grace we have forgot, nothing goes right."

FORGIVENESS

There is no greater enemy to serenity than an unforgiving nature. People offend each other; harsh things are said and done. It is not easy to keep one's temper all the time, for wrong should be resisted. The harm comes when there is no forgiveness. Paul said, "Be ye kind one to another, tender-hearted, forgiving one another, even as God for Christ's sake hath forgiven you."

Sometimes people have unknowingly offended. The older woman has much more time to dwell on what was said or done. She has less communication than the busy housewife. She may even live alone without a person close to her on whom she can

74

depend for an unbiased appraisal. To keep a healthy outlook, she must not allow herself to become over-sensitive. If a son or daughter or friend has not written, forgive the omission. If friends have not called as often as they did before, their interests may have changed to others or they may have burdens they do not wish to share at the moment. Whatever the slight, keep communications open with a forgiving spirit, thinking only the best about the offender. Nine times out of ten it is thoughtlessness.

We cannot stay offended with a person for whom we pray. Although the relationship may not visibly improve, the feeling within us will. Someone has said, "God grant me the serenity to accept the things I cannot change, the courage to change the things I can, and the sense to know the difference."

SPEECH

Our speech is very much a part of us. It is a key to our character, the revelation of our inner life. Jesus said, "Out of the abundance of the heart the mouth speaketh. . . . Every idle word that men shall speak, they shall give account thereof in the day of judgment" (Matthew 12:29, 31). We are not judged by what we say under social restraints alone but in every situation.

Words have terrifying power. They can strip a woman of a good name. They can rob her of all her effectiveness in a community. They can also heal a misunderstanding and give new life.

Words are real and can create activity toward improving or destroying. The mature woman has learned the joy of encouraging others through speech. Try this experiment for a week:

1. Express praise for the efforts of others, however small.
2. Tell the good side of any person who is mentioned.
3. Listen with patience about other's ills and do not rehearse your own.

By the end of the week you will know how to use the "good" word.

"Avoid empty and worldly chatter; those who indulge in it will stray further and further into godless courses, and the infection of their teaching will spread like a gangrene" (II Timothy 2:16, N.E.B.).

There are times for light conversation, but there are more times when depth and thoughtfulness are needed. The mature woman needs to know current events as well as other things. She should have opinions and be able to express them without being rude or outspoken. With her experience and time for self-improvement she should have a distinct contribution to offer in her conversation. She should be able to recognize gossip immediately and deftly turn it aside.

"Whatsoever things are true, whatsoever things are honest, whatsoever things are just, whatsoever things are pure, whatsoever things are lovely, whatsoever things are of good report; if there be any virtue, and if there be any praise, think on these things."— Philippians 4:8.

Paul's counsel to the Philippians is relevant to our mature woman today. Our minds are invaded with disquieting events every day when we pick up the newspaper, turn on the radio or TV. We need to know many of these things. We cannot insulate ourselves from the happenings of the world because we are very much a part of it. But if we allow our thoughts to dwell on the sensational and evil, we sacrifice our peace of mind. There was a woman whose blood pressure soared when she read irresponsible comments of certain politicians. Another woman is in constant turmoil with world affairs. We need to care, but there are happenings of good report—true, honest, pure, lovely—every day that need to be thought about and talked about.

PAUSING

A continuously hurried woman is a wearing spectacle. She probably has no more to do than her wiser counterpart, but there is a flurry and a rush surrounding her which defeat the effect of a well-organized life. Some women are so busy getting things done, they reach the end of their lives without having lived. An old spiritual says:

Slow me down, Lawd, I'se a-goin' too fast,
I can't see my brother when he's walkin'
    past,
I miss a lot o' good things day by day,
I don't know a blessing when it comes
    my way.

We must learn the pleasure of pausing. A change of pace enhances living. Our appreciation increases when we allow it to function. Some states are building bicycle paths where people can spend a leisurely vacation on the road without the fear of speeding traffic. The scenery is savored instead of passing in a continuous blur. A flower or a birdsong becomes an individual thing of beauty merely because one can slow down and be aware. It is not what there is to see or hear but how we react to it.

Pausing increases efficiency. A task may seem overwhelming, but a brief rest will help us perform more accurately because the tension is relieved. Sometimes if we deliberately turn our conscious mind away from a problem, our subconscious continues to work and we find that when we are ready to take up what we dreaded, it is already solved.

Little periods of deliberate aimlessness can bring us closer to other people. There was a woman who lived in a city which, of course, limited her property. In spite of the small space she grew six tomato plants, two rows of beans, a few roses, and a small flower garden. In the evening after work, either she or her husband would jokingly say, "Let's go look at the estate." This brief period of relaxation brought more than a view of growing things; it was a rejuvenation, a flowing back of energy lost in the pressures of the day. It brought the quiet, solemn joy of being together.

Children are excellent pausers. A walk with a child can teach us many things.

LISTENING WITH CONFIDENCE

"For ye shall not go out with haste . . . for the Lord will go before you" (Isaiah 52:12). We hurry into situations that are beyond our finite wisdom, never finishing our tasks and exhausting ourselves. We need help daily. We need the peace of God to sustain us. Morning prayer is essential in every life to bring a calm perspective to the day ahead.

Take time to be holy, let Him be thy
    guide
And run not before Him whatever betide.

"And thine ears shall hear a word behind thee, saying, This is the way, walk ye in it" (Isaiah 30:21). Guidance is not often the audible voice of God, but it may be the quickening of the intellect. It may be a word from a friend, the recollection of a hymn, a song, a poem, scripture. Whatever form it assumes, it does require a responsive spirit—a hearing ear. When we learn to pause and listen, our lives can be guided.

In a lecture at Kansas University, Arnold Toynbee made this statement: "Religion will be the treasure of freedom for mankind in the atomic age."

This is our source of confidence. When

we rely on the eternal love of God and focus on the "solemnities of eternity," our anxieties are diminished. It has been said that the more two people love each other, the less afraid one is of what the other might do to hurt him. The more we accept God's love and give ourselves in return, the more confidence we will have in the future.

"They that wait upon the Lord shall renew their strength; they shall mount up with wings as eagles; they shall run, and not be weary; and they shall walk, and not faint."—Isaiah 40:31.

CHAPTER 5 **ACHIEVEMENT AND SERVICE** SHE LAYETH HER HAND
TO THE SPINDLE
AND HER HANDS
HOLD THE DISTAFF

For age is opportunity no less
Than youth itself, though in another dress,
And as the evening twilight fades away
The sky is filled with stars, invisible by day.
—"Moriture Salutamis," LONGFELLOW

When wisdom and experience have infiltrated our character, we begin to see the "stars" which were invisible in our youth. We begin to understand better. Opportunities surround us only in "another dress." The later years were not made for vegetation, resignation, and waiting. They are a time of fulfillment, a time of achievement, a time of creativity and service.

WE ARE INDIVIDUALS

We need respect for ourselves and what we are accomplishing, not just what we have accomplished. We are still individuals who are "becoming" as individuals, competing only with our best self and no other persons. Paul wrote this advice to the Galatians (6:4, N.E.B.), "Each man should examine his own conduct for himself; then he can measure his achievement by comparing himself with himself and not with anyone else."

In the maturing years there are greater differences among people of the same age group than ever before. When we begin life as an infant, we have the influence of heredity and only a brief period of environment. As life impresses itself upon us and we react through the years, we become very complex individuals. As we experience the process of aging, there will come some disabilities, but as long as we live we always have some abilities. Our achievements from now on can be greater than ever before.

William James said the greatest revolution in his generation was the discovery that human beings, by changing the inner attitudes of their minds, can change the outer aspects of their lives.

QUALITY ACTIVITIES

Some women are "joiners." Their names appear on all the local rosters regardless of their participation. In these days communities have organizations for every imaginable interest. The wise young matron learns to guard her time and spend it in ways that will benefit her and her family and eventually the community and church. As she matures and her children leave home, she will be able to be selective in her activities. She has not "tried them all." She can put her best effort into two or three projects or organizations and make a worthwhile contribution.

When we enter into an activity, it should be done with consideration. We think in terms of what we can give as well as receive. This is a time of our lives when quality should matter more than ever before. Our work should be a symbol of excellence because by this time we should have sharpened our discernment of what is good through experience. A phrase used in modern industry is "quality control." We need to check everything we do against our established standards so that nothing inferior passes. With this built-in "quality control," we will not allow ourselves to become fragmented by every activity that looks attractive. We need to evaluate what we are doing at least every five years to measure its value in accomplishment, happiness, and progress relative to the demands on our time and energy.

BOREDOM

Some persons get up each morning with several challenges to meet during the day. Others need to create a challenge or there will be no purpose in arising. Enforced leisure can be a precious gift or a sore trial.

Boredom is sometimes difficult to overcome. This is where early training and education can be a help. We can recognize it for what it is and do something about it. It is not always a lack of "busyness." One can be in the midst of a humming household or observing the best in entertainment and still not be a part of it. Strangely enough, it is not the big things that bore us but the little things. Waiting in a doctor's office can be a very boring time. But if we are writing to a friend or reading a book, the time passes quickly.

A woman in her eighties fell and broke her shoulder. She was rushed to the hospital and placed on the X-ray table. As she lay there, she whispered continuously. The attendant asked her if she were in pain. "Oh, no," she said, "I was just composing some poetry. I always do that when I have to wait for people." Disciplining the mind is a first step in overcoming disinterest.

"At least half the sins of mankind are caused by attempts to escape boredom" (Bertrand Russell). Complete boredom can literally drive one crazy. It does not happen quickly, but when the mind and imagination are no longer stimulated, we begin to die.

Children need a dependable routine to make them feel secure, but too many women cannot change their schedule even after the family leaves the home. Their washday is still Monday; they follow the same route to the store; they have the same menus for breakfast, lunch, and dinner; they invite the same friends for the evening. Let's start changing the little routine things today. There is no room for boredom in this world of so many interesting people and things.

SHALL WE SERVE?

Sometimes a person who is successful in one line of endeavor will go no further.

She is afraid that she may lose this image and so she clasps it tightly to herself, never venturing again for fear of not measuring up to her former self. It was said of the great composer Gustave Holst, "He would never have learned so much if he had not written so many failures." It is a good feeling to be safe, but in our later years we cannot "rest on our laurels" and merely exist. There is too much to be done.

With God's help we develop our own "divine sensitivity." Our whole nature becomes aware of the needs around us as we search for ways of service. True, not every one wishes to serve others. The average is one out of three. We are well acquainted with a prime example—the story of the Good Samaritan. Persons can look the other way as easily today as they did 2,000 years ago.

But we still have the perfection of selflessness in Christ. He has shown us that we can serve and still maintain our self-respect. He "made himself of no reputation, and took upon him the form of a servant, and was made in the likeness of men" (Philippians 2:7, K.J.V.). His attitude toward service was initiated by love and maintained by love even when the tasks became unpleasant.

It is only in this same spirit that we can serve.

"Charity is the pure love of Christ, and it endureth for ever; and whoso is found possessed of it at the last day, it shall be well with them."—Moroni 7:52.

Service in the area of older women's ability can be unique. There is a depth of life's experience and understanding which can be given only by the mature woman. She is a person enriched with ability that is not studied alone, but felt, for in many instances she has a knowledge and an empathy brought about by having been there.

"Men [and women] should be anxiously engaged in a good cause, and do many things of their own free will, and bring to pass much righteousness; for the power is in them, wherein they are agents unto themselves." — Doctrine and Covenants 58:6 d.

AREAS OF SERVICE

Mrs. B had been in the hospital twice for major surgery. She had suffered pain, nausea, depression, weakness, fear, and dread. She had also known early in her marriage the concern of being a mother and the heartbreak of losing a child. Her husband had had a severe heart condition a year before his death. She had sat beside him in the ambulance on more than one occasion as they sped through the heavy traffic of a metropolitan city. She understood well the needs of the sick. Her health was good and at the age of sixty-eight she moved to a small town to be near the rest of her family. She had a new life to begin, new friends to make. Her first venture into the community was to offer her services in the local hospital as a Red Cross volunteer. She was regular in attendance, efficient, and gave that extra devotion so characteristic of an understanding heart. Her life reached into several areas—church, music, government—but her dominant interest remained in helping those who were ill. She carried an empathic concern for many persons.

Mrs. A was a lady of distinction. She had been surrounded by the good things of life from childhood. She was also taught that because of these blessings she had a responsibility to others and that she must share her talents as well as her worldly goods. Her childhood was spent in the Midwest but in her youth she had studied in France. Early in her life she accepted leadership which challenged her in several areas. Her active years were well spent. When she retired from her responsibilities, there was a continuation of counseling and encouragement. Many lives, from young children to elderly people, were affected by the example of this gracious woman. A few months before her death, she was asked to translate a visa written in the French language for one who was traveling to Tahiti. With joy for the opportunity of service, she propped some pillows around her to ease her discomfort and proceeded with the task. She served with a full heart.

Mrs. C taught school for several years. After her marriage, she continued qualifying herself in this field through further education. Later she retired, but her interest in study never dimmed. One of her daughters joined the Peace Corps and went to Peru for two years. At the end of this time she suggested that her mother could be helpful if she went to South America. Mrs. C was uncertain as to whether she was still able to teach, for it had been many years since she had stood before a class. While these doubts flitted through her mind she was asked (quite by surprise) to teach a primary class in the church school. This was her opportunity to test for herself. She found that her ability had not lessened. The main difficulty was getting in and out of the little chairs, which happens to be an occupational hazard for any grown-up teaching at this grade level.

Mrs. C was in her seventies when she went to Lima, Peru. Her knowledge of the Spanish language was limited and she was lonely at first. She was welcomed into an English-speaking school as a tutor to the Peruvian children who were having difficulty with their new language. Her greatest contribution was making friends and improving the image of the American people among the Peruvians. She went with the intent of being helpful.

Mrs. F, with four children, was widowed early in life. She reared her family well. She was active in church all her life. Many years she served as a Red Cross volunteer. She survived a serious fall in her backyard when she was past seventy years old, but returned to her activities. When she was eighty, a friend called her to take her to a meeting. She graciously declined saying, "I'm sorry, this is my day to go to Resthaven and read to some of the older people."

INFLUENCE ON YOUTH
THROUGH SERVICE

In Winnetka, Illinois, an educational experiment was tried. The older people in the community were used as volunteers to help under-achievers. These were children of average or above ability but no motivation. The helpers were mostly men who were retired and had gained knowledge over a span of years. A surgeon helped with microscope experiments. An advertising executive stimulated interest in geology and geography with his mineral collection. The intangible benefits to these children cannot be assessed nor will the results be evident for years.

This field of service is not limited to men. Mature women can also carry influences into the lives of youth. There are many young girls who are going through school on a level far below their capacity to learn who need someone to infuse a new spirit into them—not by talking alone but by spending quality time with them.

Dr. Tom Dooley wrote to a friend who had graduated from medical school. He urged him to come out to the developing nations after his internship. "Bring your gadgets and the armamentarium of drugs, to be sure, but most of all bring your human spirit. Bring your enthusiasm, your drive, your energy, your dedication . . . bring your belief in the good and the right. Bring along a sense of humor." The mature woman can bring her tools of service with her but the most important part is herself.

The homely arts of knitting, crocheting, and tatting are almost unknown to two generations. The machine has accomplished a reasonable facsimile of handwork, thus destroying an appreciation of individual creativity. Of course, there would need to be a new interpretation of these arts because of the changing times. Crocheted dollies and antimacassars would have to be replaced with today's decorating ideas. The most valued articles (commercially) and the most cherished (personally) are those with the label "handmade."

Collections of glassware, china, figurines require many years of study. Through knowledge gained by what is written and a constant seeking out—sometimes in strange places—a worthwhile collection is gathered. If a young woman were to observe these in a store or museum, she would not share the feeling of personal attachment, but working with an individual, she will sense the need of research, of history, of close scrutiny of detail. Above all she will gain an appreciation which in turn stimulates a love of learning.

A current article in the newspaper pleads for help in the Head Start program. Some children do not know how to carry on an ordinary conversation. Others have never learned to wash their hands and faces. The influence of a normal life has never been experienced by these children, and when they begin school they are far behind the average child of school age. This is an important area in which we can assist. These children have been thrown on their own resources with a very thin and inadequate background.

We possess many gifts which we have assumed to be ours. We may feel that we have earned them. But

"Are we not all beggars? Do we not all depend upon the same . . . God? Now, if God, who has created you, on whom you are dependent for your lives and for all that you have and are, grants to you whatever you ask that is right, in faith, believing that you shall receive, oh, then, how had you ought to impart of the substance that you have, one to another?"—Mosiah 2:32, 36.

We have no right to hoard, for we have received numberless gifts and ideas which we did not particularly merit. Jesus said (John 4:38, N.E.B.), "I sent you to reap a crop for which you have not toiled. Others toiled and you have come in for the harvest of their toil." We may not reap what we have sown, but others may. We need to share ourselves.

SENIOR CITIZENS GROUPS

One's choice of activity is an individual thing. Golden Age or Senior Citizens groups are giving incentive for living to many persons throughout the country. The programs for a monthly luncheon meeting are planned by the members. They include current topics of interest, including their city and county government, with talks by candidates for office. One group has its own orchestra and a quartet of voices. The singers are all over seventy. Last year forty senior citizens traveled through Europe together. Next year they are planning another tour.

Traveling by boat takes time and some would like to fly one way so as to be able to have more time in a foreign land. To alleviate the fear of those who have not experienced flying, a short trip has been planned by an airline to encourage them in this venture.

The activities are not all social. Members serve in the hospital by rolling bandages, making place mats, and many other small but necessary tasks.

As was mentioned before, what we do with our time and which circles we desire to move in depend on us. The senior citizens group is a help, a need, an inspiration to many older persons; but do not be dismayed if it does nothing for you. All through life we find there are some who prefer something different from the group. Humanity is this way. Be thankful.

BE CREATIVE

André Gide, Nobel Prize winner, gives this advice not only to writers and painters and sculptors but to every member of the human race who wishes to fulfill the purpose of his being born into this world at this time:

"Look for your own. Do not do what someone else could do as well as you. Do not say, do not write, what someone else could say, could write as well as you. Care for nothing in yourself but what you feel exists nowhere else—and out of yourself create, impatiently or patiently . . . the most irreplaceable of beings."—From *Educated Heart*.

These years have been allowed us for a reason. If we were of no use to God's creation after we reached the age of forty or fifty—if, like some insects, we were meant simply to reproduce our kind and die—that is what would have happened. As it is, we have our experience and the ability to use that to further seek our purpose for being here during this particular span of time. We do not lose our creativity at a certain age; rather it is enhanced if it has been used. If we had it as a child, we still have it. It may be lying dormant within us, waiting to be reawakened. Our years of home responsibility have not allowed us the time to explore, but now with our wealth of experience we have more material than ever before.

Much of the finest writing through the ages was done by people who had retired.

Many great treasures of art and music were created in the latter years of life when tensions were lifted. This is a time when we can pursue our partially developed talents or—as many persons have done—strike out in an entirely different direction. First we must study our interests and abilities. One discipline carries over into another field whether the subject is related or not.

THE WELL KNOWN

We have read of the remarkable contributions of persons like Dr. Fleming who discovered penicillin when he was seventy; Maestro Toscanini who brilliantly conducted the symphony when past eighty; Grandma Moses whose paintings became famous although she began at the age of seventy; Robert Frost who continued writing his poetry when past eighty; Herbert Hoover who served his country when in his eighties; Igor Stravinsky who shocked music circles with his "Rite of Spring" ballet generations ago and who is now experimenting with a new form of music. These have all been compulsive workers who could never satisfy their yearning for perfection and new challenge.

NOT SO WELL KNOWN

The creative avenues for the average woman are numerous. Thousands of middle-aged women without any previous experience have successfully organized small businesses. This provides a great satisfaction even though the profits may be small. One woman can manage a shop of knitting and wool, antiques, lingerie, hats, gifts, or services such as telephone answering, stenographic work, and baby-sitting.

If you have an interest, explore it fully. A woman began working crossword puzzles. She found that her vocabulary was limited but it improved with practice. She transferred this knowledge to writing and started a successful career in her sixties.

Some skills can increase indefinitely; photography, ceramics, needlework. Women have become experts on herbs, flowers, and growing things.

A gift of a pair of warblers started a woman in a study of their care and breeding. She sold birds. Another woman received a gift of a small loom which led to a satisfying hobby of weaving.

NOW IS THE TIME

We have been given additional years and healthy bodies with which to live them. Probably our greatest sin against these gifts is procrastination. We find difficulty in "overcoming the dead lift"—making that first move. We think we will start next week, sometime—and we postpone "ad infinitum."

"Arise therefore, and be doing, and the Lord be with thee" (I Chronicles 22:16).

A personal credo written by Dr. F. M. McDowell was published in the *Saints' Herald* of August 15, 1955, called "Confessions of a Senior Adult." It reads:

I am going to try to:

Keep affirmative in attitude and in conversation

Keep growing

Keep forward looking, expectant

Maintain a zest for living

Keep on learning by study and by faith

Try to expect new and better things

Accept the fact that I am older

Seek to be realistic and honest with myself

Act my age and be proud of it

Keep the pathway open to God and my fellowmen

Discover substitute activities and interests to replace those I have had to relinquish

Keep my eyes focused on longtime goals. Yonder lies the kingdom. God has set his hand to that task and I have; he is going to keep on working at it and by the grace of God, I am going to keep on working at it

Try to set up some immediate achievable goals

Find renewed joys in the pursuits and achievements of the gospel way

Keep on seeking life in terms of God's eternal purposes

Try to emulate the example of the one who did so well himself. "Forgetting what lies behind and straining forward to what lies ahead, I press on toward the goal for the prize of the upward call of God in Christ Jesus."

CHAPTER 6   **FAMILY RELATIONS**   HER CHILDREN
RISE UP AND CALL
HER BLESSED

A woman's later years bring further developments which necessitate new adjustments in her relations to others. Situations have changed between her and her husband, her children, her parents, and her friends. If she is very fortunate she has grandchildren to add to her circle.

Previous to 1900, the average woman became a widow before her last child left home. Today it is probable that she will have the companionship of her husband for at least fourteen years after their children leave. The reasons for this are the following: there are fewer children, they come earlier in marriage, and advances in medicine and living conditions have greatly extended man's life expectancy.

BACK TO TWO IN THE HOME

This companionship in later years can be a harvesttime and a growing time. Each partner needs to be aware of the shortness of this period and to treasure and savor it without fearing its termination. A deep sensitivity to each other's needs and a desire to lift and sustain should predominate in each life.

"Every wise woman buildeth her house; but the foolish plucketh it down with her hands."—Proverbs 14:1, I.V.

Now more than ever, home should be a desirable place—a place of encouragement, of reassurance and appreciation. After the children leave, refurbish the home for couple-living. Give Dad that large, comfortable extra bedroom for his study rather than a corner that everyone uses. Rework your kitchen and each room in the house for easier upkeep. Pretend you are just moving in as a couple and use your imagination. Invest your time, energy, and resources wisely to make your home a worthwhile abode not only for you and your husband but for those who visit you.

Conversation must go well beyond the neighbor's dog or the news broadcast to keep a marriage alive. A scheduled plan of daily reading is a necessity to bring new areas of thought into discussion. A wife must learn to initiate interesting ideas and be knowledgeable on several subjects to make communication a stimulating part of life.

This is a time to find pleasure in joint activities. New hobbies can be developed together: antique collecting, photography, lapidary, gardening, coin collecting, bird watching. Vacations can be taken any time of the year thus avoiding the tourist rush. Community projects can be supported: political movements, drives for worthwhile projects such as a new library or an orchestra.

NO ROOM FOR BLAME

There was once a small boy who whenever he made a mistake or broke anything immediately shouted, "See what you made me do!" A mature woman always looks at her marriage partner with eyes of appreciation. She praises him and does not blame, for there is always much to praise if she looks for it. When we appreciate a person we ourselves prosper, but when we belittle we lose. A marriage is better when we have freedom of knowing we will not be censured for every error.

"It is better to live in a desert land than with a contentious and fretful woman."— Proverbs 21:19, R.S.V.

This is not a new problem, but when physical attractiveness wanes, there had better be some beauty of spirit to offset this decline or the result is a very lonely old woman. It is sad to see an older woman with a querulous disposition. To understand how she became that way involves a long study of her background from infancy.

The pattern of living together is quite firmly established in twenty-five years. By this time a woman knows what pleases her husband and what irritates him. She can accurately predict what he will say and what he will do under certain circumstances. With this vast store of knowledge, she is capable of making these later years more livable, more exciting, more interesting than ever before.

IF DEATH COMES

"One very hard adjustment which comes sooner or later to nearly every woman is the death of her husband. The average woman becomes a widow before seventy; the average man, however, is not a widower until eighty-five, if he lives that long. Never until this experience comes to you can you realize why the scriptures speak so often in mercy and pity of the widow; 'Blessed are they that mourn, for they shall be comforted' takes on a far deeper significance than before. This does not refer to the loud, incessant clack of the professional mourner of oriental times; it is the quiet, ever present grief, sweetened and made tolerable only by that abiding peace that faith can bring. As you accept your lot you receive a deeper sense of the blessing of divine Presence than you have known before.

"But there come physical adjustments and changes and problems that try your soul when you lose your husband. You have to learn to transact business matters. You usually have to try to manage on a depleted income. You may have to live alone. You may have to move out of the gracious house, made especially dear by years of blessed associations, and reduce your furniture and possessions to a much smaller space. You may have to choose between a rooming house or moving in with relatives or your children. God help you—and I say it reverently—and he will. In proportion as you meet these problems with faith and courage, your life becomes richer than ever before and your Savior nearer. You accept your lot, learn to knock on new doors of mental and spiritual discovery and adventure. You go on building by your life a true memorial to your loved one as you keep faith day by day with the ideals you two formulated and lived by in your years together."

These words are from the article "Years of Fulfillment" written by Mrs. S. A. Burgess, and published in the *Saints' Herald* of July 12, 1954.

NEW ROLES TO FILL

A woman faces a complex emotional situation as she approaches her middle and later years. After twenty years or more of managing a family, she must divert her thoughts, love, and activity to other ways so that the new family unit may establish its own identity.

Setting young adults free is a difficult task. One mother sent her son in the university a birthday gift when he was twenty-one. Imagine his surprise to find two lovely, starched, organdy apron strings. He was no longer tied to her and this was her humorous reminder.

BEING A MOTHER-IN-LAW

The relationship of mother-in-law to son or daughter is considered the most difficult of all. Every woman wishes to be exceptional in this role for the sake of the family unit. She desires a close, warm, friendly relationship without being in the way. Mother-in-law jokes have been less popular in recent years but the tradition persists. Tension can be aggravated or reduced by those in both generations who are involved. It has been said that if you have loved your children's playmates and friends through the years because they loved them, then the position of mother-in-law is easier.

It is possible to have good companionship with the young woman who now represents the major part of your son's life. You also may achieve new perspectives and interests with the young man who has assumed the responsibility of caring for your daughter. These relationships probably will exist all your life so it is worth your time and effort to make them as wholesome and pleasant as possible.

NAOMI AND RUTH

The most beautiful story ever told of a mother-in-law and daughter-in-law association is found in the Book of Ruth. Throughout the narrative, Naomi unselfishly plans and acts for the welfare of her daughters-in-law. After her sons' deaths she urges the daughters-in-law to leave her and find husbands with their own people. Orpah obeys but Ruth has a deeper concern for her, expressing it in this scripture of human devotion:

"Entreat me not to leave thee, or to return from following after thee; for whither thou goest, I will go; and where thou lodgest, I will lodge; thy people shall be my people, and thy God my God. Where thou diest, will I die, and there will I be buried; the Lord do so to me, and more also, if aught but death part thee and me."—Ruth 1:16, 17.

Later, when Ruth marries Naomi's kinsman Boaz, they have a son. At the birth of Obed, the women said, "Thy daughter-in-law, which loveth thee, which is better to thee than seven sons, hath borne him" (Ruth 4:15).

This is a classic of two women in separate generations who surmounted a difficult relationship. They understood each other and trusted each other. Each was sensitive to the needs of the other.

GIVE AND TAKE

A successful marriage or friendship requires unselfish interaction. Different generations working together as relatives need to be flexible. This is not a one-sided affair. There will be times when we can do a favor and there will be times when we need one. If a mother-in-law insists upon sacrificing herself and refusing help, her martyr complex will begin to show, thus negating the good she is trying to do.

DECISIONS

When your child marries he and his wife or she and her husband have a right to make their own decisions; where they shall live, how they spend their money, and in all their personal matters.

Too many times we have seen the well-intentioned mother-in-law make choices for her children "for their own good." Experience teaches us many things, but the generation we are trying to advise has learned in a different time, and they must spread their wings to be able to fly. A gentle nudge occasionally (not too many) may set things in proper focus, but the major decisions are to be made by the married couple.

THEY ARE A UNIT

We have heard the statement, "I did not lose a daughter [or son], I gained a son [or daughter]." If we can approach our child's marriage with this attitude and maintain it through the years, we are on safe ground. The young person will be a part of the family and the marriage will be a unit.

When we speak of them, we will say, "John and Susan" rather than "my son John and his wife Susan."

We must keep our conversation above reproach and not say anything to one that we would not want the other to hear. If the marriage is sound, the comment will eventually be told to the other partner anyway. When your son or daughter marries you no longer have your child to yourself; you have a husband-wife combination.

CREATING BAD FEELINGS

This statement was made, "A mother never feels that her son or daughter married

111

the person equal to him or her." This is not always true, as many mothers can testify. But we do tend to see faults in others more quickly if our attitude is not loving toward them. That is why we continue to forgive our children and look critically upon the partners they have chosen. We are also prone to judge a marriage when we see only the surface.

We may happen to hear a chance remark of no particular significance between a couple and attach the wrong meaning. Many misunderstandings can be quickly overcome without the "judgment" of the third party stirring up the situation. Let's take a walk when we see the storm gathering.

"Blessed are the peacemakers." A mother-in-law who agitates is seldom welcome in a family.

DO NOT TRY TO MAKE THEM OVER

Your daughter-in-law or son-in-law may have come from the same social level and have the same education and general beliefs as your child, but the family background and disposition are different.

If your daughter-in-law keeps your beautiful little granddaughter in jeans, constant pressure will not remedy this. Perhaps the frilly dresses you bought her are difficult to iron, or perhaps her mother does not consider femininity a special asset to be learned from childhood.

Find the good attributes like the mother-in-law who viewed her son-in-law's untidy work bench. "He is trying—very trying, but he is a wonderful father. He never misses an overnight hike with the Scouts or a school activity. He encourages every member of the family in worthwhile endeavors."

A mother-in-law can occasionally suggest and even be allowed to help, but unless the young person wishes to change, and is teachable, advice and example will be lost.

REFRAIN FROM COMPARISONS

When your grandson misbehaves, your daughter-in-law does not want to hear from you about the good manners of his cousin. There is something about a comparison that not only cuts the ego but also destroys the possible good relationship that could exist between the two persons compared.

A son-in-law's confidence can be severely injured by commenting on his abilities as a provider for your daughter.

He is probably doing his best to succeed. If their home is not as pretentious as others, or they decide to spend their vacation at home, they have their reasons. Comparisons with others are never helpful.

REFRAIN FROM GOSSIP

The old saying "A dog that brings a bone will take one away" is applicable in family relationships.

If a mother-in-law reports from household to household or, worse yet, to casual friends, incidents such as Susie's tantrums or John's moodiness or the failures in scholarship or business, she will soon experience a coolness and withdrawal of her children. They can be certain that what they do or say will be carried to someone else.

If this habit should start developing, discipline it. But like the man who swept and garnished his house, you cannot leave a vacuum or you will be in worse trouble than before (Luke 11:24). Involve yourself in worthwhile activity; read, study. In this way you will have better and more interesting things to discuss. Our children need to have confidence in us. They need that comfortable assurance of freedom in our presence, knowing that we have the wisdom to discern what is not to be mentioned again.

A TWO-WAY STREET?

Everything possible should be done to make the mother-in-law and daughter-in-law relationship a good experience. Occasionally we see mothers who apparently are blameless but cannot surmount the difficulties. Four reasons are given by Edith G. Neisser in her Public Affairs Pamphlet "How to Be a Good Mother-in-law and Grandmother" as to why you may be resented as a mother-in-law in spite of your conduct.

1. Sometimes a mother is still competition for her daughter-in-law. This is particularly true when the mother-in-law is well established and well liked in a community and the daughter is a stranger.

2. A husband or wife may feel that his or her mate was never understood or appreciated as a child—a brother or sister was favored more.

3. All shortcomings of the spouse are the fault of the mother for not giving better training.

4. A mother-in-law is used as a scapegoat. The young person may have disliked his or

her own mother but felt guilty about it. These unnatural feelings were not acceptable so were transferred to the mother-in-law.

IS THERE A SOLUTION?

The crux of this relationship is that two persons have a strong love for one person. This can be made an advantage or the reverse. If the love is Christlike or sacrificial, it will be wise, wholesome, and aware of every need of that person. It will encompass the person without possessing him. It will hold dear those persons whom he regards as precious.

The apostle Paul gave some thoughtful rules about love which are appropriate to our mother-in-law and daughter-in-law (or son-in-law) relationship today when he said:

"Love is patient; love is kind and envies no one. Love is never boastful, nor conceited, nor rude; never selfish, not quick to take offence. Love keeps no score of wrongs; does not gloat over other men's sins, but delights in the truth. There is nothing love cannot face; there is no limit to its faith, its hope, and its endurance."— I Corinthians 13:4-8, N.E.B.

OLDER PARENTS

In the middle years, it is usual to have aging parents. Two generations ago, families were inclined to stay in the same section of the country, but today we find them scattered to every point of the compass. This may pose problems for parents as they grow older. They still have basic needs which closely parallel those who are in their teens:

1. Independence
2. Privacy
3. A place for personal possessions
4. Affection
5. Respect

Older people should be allowed to remain in their own homes as long as they can possibly manage it. This is their "castle," an essential part of their physical and psychological freedom.

Too often when a spouse dies, the children superintend the liquidating of the home so that mother or father can come and live with them. This may be best in some cases, but in most, it is a cruel upheaval in the life of the one concerned. Let the mother or father pay an extended visit to the prospective "new home." Perhaps he or she will be lonely in your neighborhood. It is quite possible the grandchildren will not be the "darlings" they were on an occasional visit. The "in-law" relationship may be a constant strain because of being too close. Give it a fair trial before making a decision.

A son or daughter is wise to help the parent be self-sustaining. If a mother is arthritic or in ill health, try to find a visiting housekeeper to help with heavier work. Some communities have organized a service in which a woman comes in perhaps twice a week for an hour or two and takes care of any small need not requiring professional help (cleaning, or preparing a hot meal). This organization of qualified women is also an opportunity for employment for older able-bodied women whose children are grown.

We sometimes are too careful of older persons when a little "fling" might be the psychological lift that they need. Sons and daughters must not put parents under glass to preserve them if they are capable of making their own decisions. They may feel obligated to obey you, but they may also feel cheated.

A woman answered her doorbell one winter morning and found her seventy-five-year-old-mother standing there smiling like a child with a surprise. She had walked almost a mile through the falling snow and the large flakes clung to her clothing. Her face was alive with enthusiasm and pleasure. She was aware of the hazards of slipping, but the pure enjoyment of that walk at that particular time was not to be denied. Caution is desirable, but too many restrictions make life very drab.

If financial circumstances dictate that a parent cannot keep a separate household, arrangements will have to be made to live with the children. Before entering into this, an understanding should be had in advance. If possible, the parent should have a room of her own with some of her own furnishings. Her privacy should be completely respected. If you are wholly supporting your parent, she should have a small amount of pocket money for spending as she pleases. Do not reprove if you feel it is spent unwisely. There will be problems, but if a parent is used to managing and carries this into your home, the best solution is to encourage outside activities where this ability can be expended and probably appreciated.

It is possible for two generations to be acquainted with the same people, but it is not good to share the same social affairs and friends all the time. Too many times a daughter has been sacrificed by the thoughtless possessiveness of a mother who had to be included in every gathering. On the other hand, parents should be encouraged to visit with their old friends and make new ones.

If the time should come that parents need professional care, the decision should be made for the good of all concerned—the parent or parents, their daughter or son and spouse, and the grandchildren. Selection of a home is an intensely personal affair. We must be guided by the heart as well as the head. We must be convinced that this is the best way to "Honor thy father and thy mother." Even so there will be feelings of guilt. It is well to talk with those who have parents in a nursing home. Make a list of reputable homes in your area and visit them unannounced. The operators will give references with whom you should talk.

One authority has said, "If I were seeking a nursing home in which to place a relative, the first thing I would investigate would be the operator's attitude."

Beautiful surroundings and an extensive staff are desirable, but it is most important that the operator is dedicated and can give adequate nursing care to the individuals. The director should be well informed on the latest advances in gerontology and implement the ideas as soon as possible.

Whatever the circumstances, whether the parent is independent and living alone, or staying with children, or in a nursing home, there is a vital need for love, affection, and respect. Some parents become very unlovely as they grow older. We may not understand the "thorn" that has caused the change of disposition and we are not in a position to judge.

GRANDMOTHER

Under usual circumstances, by the time we have reached our fiftieth birthday we are grandmothers. This does not mean we are over the hill and on the downward path. Rather we are climbing upward into new experiences which can be appreciated only by maturity. With the advent of our children's children, there are new lives which we can enrich with wisdom and love. We gather our good experiences about us and seek to grow in this new relationship. We have a contribution to make to each child— a gift of faith, godliness, love, patience, and righteousness. A consecrated grandmother can leave a heritage to be remembered a lifetime and an influence which reaches far into the future.

A child never has too much of the right kind of love. It is essential to his emotional health. A grandmother can supplement the love of the parents and still never spoil the child. He must be taken as he is with warmth and spontaneity.

A small child's world is increased when he finds grandmother as receptive to him as his own mother. He learns to trust other people outside his immediate family. Later he finds that grandmother's home, as well as his own familiar environment, is a place where he can be safe and happy. There are times when he will want an adult all to himself without the competition of other brothers and sisters. He likes to feel special. Grandmother can provide this haven.

He also discovers there is more than one way to do something. Grandmother would rather you did not run and jump down the stairs. Mother does not mind. On the other hand, Grandmother's cookie jar is conveniently placed within reach on the kitchen cupboard—eat one when you want it. Mother's cookies are out of sight and there are specific times when you may have one. If he tells you he likes the chocolate milk the way his mother prepares it better than yours, remember he is probably praising the pancakes you gave him to his mother.

A grandmother needs an understanding of present-day principles of child development. The pendulum swings forth and back in each generation. Twenty-five years ago we were not supposed to rock a baby. Now we do. Baby food was all strained and the junior foods were not yet invented, so the child ate strained foods until he had enough teeth to chew the solids. Today, with a little guidance, the baby establishes his own pattern of eating and sleeping which was the method two generations ago. It is wise for us as grandmothers to know about the current principles of child raising. If our grandchildren's parents subscribe to these new ideas, we should support them also. It is one source of conflict we can avoid.

REFRAIN FROM CRITICISM

It is difficult to stand by and watch young parents take a course of action which may be a mistake. Each generation will err in a different direction. The course of action our children choose will probably not end in any more of a catastrophe than some of the choices we made at their age.

One young woman's first serious disciplining of her older son occurred when he insisted upon taking the plates and silver off the table and putting them on the floor. She was preparing dinner and this extra work became wearing. He received his first spanking. Later she wrote to his two grandmothers and mentioned the incident. The return mail was immediate and the letters were classics which she placed in his baby book. Both grandmothers knew the need of discipline and tried not to scold her, but they were hurt when their grandson was spanked. One closed by saying, "Perhaps you had better not tell me this kind of experience again." This young mother was fortunate to have perfect grandmothers for her family. They were deeply concerned but tried to refrain from criticism.

AN AVOCATION

Being a grandmother should not be a career. Our love and concern will not shrink if we do not spend all our spare time with our grandchildren. In fact, it will be better for us and them if we regard this

role as an avocation. We can be detached—
or at least pretend to be—and refrain from
constantly advising on every subject. Grandmothers need not be imposed upon. Regardless of what others say, we know the limits
of our endurance. We know how much we
want to give.

POOR LITTLE GRANDMOTHER

The old rocking chair is empty today
For Grandma is no longer in it.
She is off in her car to her office or shop
And buzzes around every minute.
No one shoves Grandma back on the
    shelf.
She is versatile, forceful, dynamic.
That is not a pie in the oven, my dear—
Her baking today is ceramic.
You won't see her trundling off early to
    bed
From her place in a warm chimney nook;
Her typewriter clickety clacks through the
    night
For Grandma is writing a book.
She is not content with crumbs of old
    thoughts,
With meager and second-hand knowl-
    edge—

Don't bring your mending for Grandma
   to do
For Grandma has gone back to college.
                        —Author unknown

A SPECIAL ROLE

The statement was made, "Grandmothers
are mothers who have time."

They have time to take a slow walk while
the child stops to examine a stone or fuzzy
caterpillar; time to visit on the telephone
and listen to the latest development on the
pet tadpole; time to watch the animals in
the zoo; time to thoroughly explore a toy
department.

Grandmothers love and admire: "Doesn't
Stevie read well?" "How pretty Anne looks
with her new hairstyle." "Did you notice
how neat David's room is?" "Have you
heard Nancy play her new piece on the
piano? It is wonderful."

Grandmothers have had many experiences
and are able to sift the important from the
trivial. They can cope with the catastrophes
of youth. They can say to the five-year-old
whose friends have run away from her, leaving a vast emptiness in her small life, "That
happened to me too when I was a little girl,

but you will find other playmates. Let's do something together now and they will be back."

Grandmother's house is a special place. She has pictures of Daddy when he was a little boy and Granddaddy when he had hair. There is a wren house hanging by the window and a tree to climb.

Grandmother is the link to the past, giving continuity to family relationships and keeping the traditions alive in her presence.

CONTINUITY IN GENERATIONS

A series of interviews was made by a newspaper to determine what teen-agers fret about in their private moments. It was a surprise to learn of their concern about relations with their grandparents. They want grandparents similar to those children had fifty years ago. They feel that something is missing. They are lonely and searching for identity; they want to know why they are on earth and where they are going. Very few have had the experience of large family gatherings to ease the feeling of isolation. The teen-ager's interest in grandparents is a hope of finding continuity and purpose in life.

In avoiding the problems of too close proximity between generations, we have sacrificed a needful relationship between grandchildren and grandparents. Pearl Buck blamed much of the delinquency on the "tendency to separate generations." She said the American people are a lonely people because of the self-imposed isolation of the generations, the breakdown of close family ties.

FOR THE WELL-BEING OF ALL

Recently a friend returned to her native Australia after several years' absence. The death of her husband occurred shortly after they were settled, but she is surrounded by a loving family. She wrote of her grandchildren:

"I have had the children one at a time— here I get to know them and show them some of the ways of doing things. They appreciate sitting and talking of their little aspirations. Matthew, a handsome little guy of 11 years last, worked in the yard like a little man. He built me a rockery garden and together we cemented the water-washed stones around. He had hunted them for me in the mountains where they live. I enjoyed a real love letter from him last week. He said they were singing a soft song at school and his voice broke, tears ran down his face because he thought of me. They all love me and I must hang on to this."

The influence of a good grandmother is a precious blessing of life. Paul recognized this as he wrote to Timothy, "I am reminded of the sincerity of your faith, a faith which was alive in Lois your grandmother and Eunice your mother before you, and which, I am confident, lives in you also" (II Timothy 1:5, N.E.B.).

"Remember that from early childhood you have been familiar with the sacred writings which have power to make you wise and lead you to salvation through faith in Christ Jesus."—II Tomothy 3:15, N.E.B.

A grandmother has a special role to play in the lives of her grandchildren. We sing this hymn, with words written by W. Charter Piggott, which expresses the high desires of the good grandmother:

That we may open doors on life,
And share the visions that we see
Of the deep wonder of the world

And man's heroic history,
And wake in them the answering chord:
Give us the skill and patience, Lord.

—*The Hymnal,* No. 479

BIBLIOGRAPHY

Creative Years—Howe—$3.50 cloth; $2.00 paper (Seabury Press)

The Divine Purpose in Us—Edwards—$3.00 cloth; $2.00 paper (Herald House)

Family Development—Evelyn Duvall—$6.95 (Lippincott Press)

Outwitting Your Years—Lieb—$3.95 (Association Press)

The Potential of Woman—Farber-Wilson—$7.50 cloth; $2.95 paper (McGraw)

Seven Ages of Woman—Parker—$6.50 cloth; 95c paper (John Hopkins)

Stay Young Longer—Clark—$4.95 (Devin Press)

The Abingdon Bible Commentary—Lewis-Downey

Doctrine and Covenants

Book of Mormon
The Interpreter's Bible

Bibles

Inspired Version
King James Version
New English Bible—$4.95 cloth; $1.45 paper
Revised Standard Version

The Best Years of Your Life—Marie B. Ray
Create Your Own Tomorrow—Johnstone
The Better Half of Your Life—Lerrigo
If You Would Be Happy—Stout
Lessons for Life—Kahns (Out of print)
Living Your Later Years—Walker
Longer Life—Soule
The Road to Confidence—Rosenburg (Out of print)
The Second Forty Years—E. J. Stieglitz
Treatise on Old Age—Cicero
Youth After Forty—Allen

Public Affairs Pamphlets (22 E. 38th St., N. Y. 16—Order from this address.)
Hart, Evelyn. *Making the Most of Your Years*, No. 276
Lawton and Stewart. *When You Grow Older*, No. 131

Neisser, Edith G. *How to Be a Good Mother-in-law and Grandmother*, No. 174

Ogg, Elizabeth. *When Parents Grow Old*, No. 208

Stern, Edith M. *A Full Life After 65*, No. 347

Public Affairs Pamphlets (381 Park Ave. South, N. Y. 10016—Order from this address.)

Close, Kathryn, *Getting Ready to Retire*, No. 182

Milt, Harry. *Middle Age—Threat or Promise?* No. 294

Osborne, Ernest. *When You Lose a Loved One*, No. 269

————

*Not available from Herald House